Wildflowers in

A

Illustrations by
Tessa Lovatt-Smith

Contents

SGC Books

Herb-rich meadows may contain 30 or more different wild flowers per square metre.

At least 400 different creatures may depend on oak trees for their survival.

Some mixed hedgerows have existed for 500 years - since the reign of Henry VIII.

It is a sad fact that for many of us, especially if living in towns and cities, the chance of encountering the natural world in our daily lives becomes less and less. The British countryside is shrinking daily - how many green field sites near you have been *developed* during the last year? How many of those special childhood dells still survive?

The truth is that most of us have to go in search of wildflowers (and the creatures they nurture) in nature reserves, national parks, on holiday in Scotland or Wales - but it does not have to be so. If we all encourage the countryside, bringing it into our gardens instead of removing every trace, we won't have to search for our heritage - instead we can see it and be inspired by it, every day.

To be successful, a garden for wildflowers has to be carefully planned, the right species selected and the balance of nature created, in however small an area you have available. A shady corner left *abandoned* does not constitute a wildflower area - just a tangle of nettles, docks and thistles of some benefit to wildlife perhaps, but not very attractive to the eye.

Your garden may need a lawn for children and dogs, a rose bed for table flowers, a vegetable plot for the taste of freshness, a flower border for sheer joy - but perhaps you can also spare some areas where wildflowers might be established.

In this book we show you how to develop these areas of your garden (however modest) in a more *natural* way, making them attractive to you and to wildlife. You may have problem soil, excessive shade, an unimaginative design - giving garden plants little chance of success. But nature adapts well to such places and by following a few rules you will be surprised - perhaps delighted - by the results.

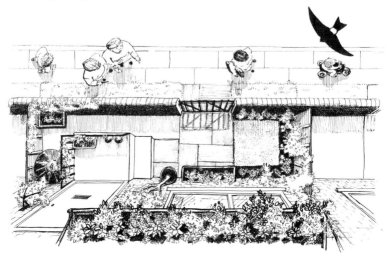

All gardens contain some shady areas - where the sun only reaches for a short while each day. These areas are typically along the north side of the house or garden , at the base of a large hedge, or under large deciduous (leaf-shedding) trees and corners which get only morning or evening sun. By choosing the right trees, shrubs and wildflowers, these areas - however small - can be turned into one of the most rewarding of wildlife habitats, the *woodland edge.*

In a natural wood

Walk in any deciduous woodland and you will find that the most bird and insect activity and the most plant life occurs around the edges of the paths, clearings and glades. Although you may not have room for large trees, by the use of one or two woodland edge trees and shrubs (which tend to be more suited to the average garden) you can fairly easily create your own piece of woodland and so gain the benefit of associated wildlife.

Spring and early summer are the periods when woodland is most colourful as many woodland plants flower early to obtain the benefit of winter and spring sunshine which reaches the ground only when the branches are bare of leaves. At other times of the year the plants survive on food in the form of sugars and starches, made during the spring and stored in underground stems, tubers, bulbs and corms. Many woodland flowers send out runners above and just below ground enabling them to colonise large areas quickly, utilizing all the available space. Luckily, most woodland flowers adapt well to a garden lifestyle.

Under the specimen tree

If you are lucky enough to have a mature tree in the garden this section is for you. Otherwise, plant one and wait for 30 years...

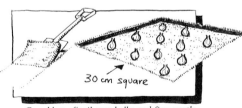

Crumble turf/soil over bulbs and firm gently

The ground under a large single tree is often very dry, shaded and devoid of plant growth. Ordinary lawn grass cannot tolerate these conditions and therefore becomes very patchy and unsightly. The usual answer to this is spring bulbs. For example, we created a *bulb garden* in a 6m circle under a very large lime tree by planting various native species. **Bluebells, snowdrops, wild daffodil, winter aconite, snakeshead fritillary** and **wood anemone** are all suitable,and are available as bulbs or corms for autumn planting.

The older the bulb when you buy it, the more likely you will get a flower the first spring, but be warned - truly native bulbs and corms are expensive, and keep them away from mice! Plant as many as you can afford and remember they flower at different times - **snowdrops** and **aconites** as early as January/February, **wild daffodils** and **wood anemones** in March/April, and **bluebells** and **fritillaries** in April/May.

With a little work - and using a wider variety of woodland plants -a *mini woodland* can become a feature all year round and be a positive haven for wildlife. Unless your tree is a large **beech** or **sycamore** (when some selective pruning may be necessary) most small garden trees allow a dappled shade to reach the ground, even in summer. First check your soil. It is likely to be dry and starved of nutrients and so for the best results it is worth improving it with a layer of leaf mould, garden compost and/or bark chippings.

If a motley collection of *weeds* - **nettles, docks, chickweed, creeping thistle, willowherb** - have found a home under the tree, remove them first. They will only be a continuing problem if you do not. (Although such *weeds* are actually important for wildlife, there are other places for them.) Define your area and make a simple plan on paper. It does not have to be symmetrical around the tree and can extend beyond the canopy. Join with an existing border or include a solid barrier such as a wall or fence in your design. Try not to let grass creep back into your woodland border - you should find the selected plants cover the ground quite quickly.

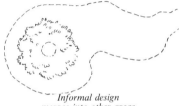

Formal design
following the canopy
of the tree

Formal design
leading to a well shaped
wildflower border

Informal design
merges into other areas
like a wildflower meadow or pond

The wildflowers shown here are suitable for most situations. If you are unsure which woodland flowers to choose, treat yourself to a visit to your nearest woodland nature reserve in spring or early summer - your County Naturalist Trust will help you with this. You will then see the plants that grow well in your area. When you have made your choice, buy pot-grown plants, as woodland flower seeds are very difficult to germinate. Give your plants an initial spacing of 30cm.

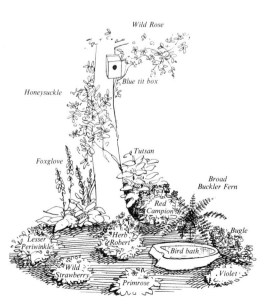

Wild Rose

Blue tit box

Honeysuckle

Foxglove

Tutsan

Broad
Buckler Fern

Red
Campion

Bugle

Lesser
Periwinkle

Herb
Robert

Bird bath

Wild
Strawberry

Primrose

Violet

To keep your woodland border neat, cut down dead stems in the autumn (or leave some seed heads for the birds and cut down in early spring) and divide perennials after a year or two's growth . Add a small bird bath (for the small birds!) and a few well placed logs to add that final touch. BUT beware - check that the logs are free from honey fungus. This is one of the most dangerous parasites of trees, causing an intensive white rot and ultimately death of your trees - and eventually your neighbours' (trees! that is). Tell-tale signs are black cords resembling bootlaces which are found beneath the bark of infected logs. The fruiting body is seen in dense clusters on and around trunks and stumps of trees and is always dark-honey coloured and mushroom shaped. The only good point of this fungus is that it is supposed to be edible after cooking...

Damp shady corners

These are typical features of ancient woodlands where ferns, mosses and other mystical plants grow alongside streams, in waterlogged hollows, rock crevices etc. If your garden has areas where the water table is high making it permanently damp, a shady stream or a particularly dark north side of a fence or wall, you could try some of these plants.

Ferns are ideal in these situations and most will thrive in deep shade, but make sure the soil is damp and shady for them most of the time - planting them by a stream, at the base of fences and walls, or even in holes in the wall (push some compost in with them as you plant). Place some natural stone or logs between them and watch the **mosses, liverworts** and **fungi** move in.

The **ferns** shown here are particularly suitable for the *damp* situation and are usually available from good garden centres. Just follow the instructions on the label - they should soon feel at home and look after themselves. You will be surprised at how much wildlife will be attracted to this area: frogs, toads, newts and small birds will quickly discover this new feeding station.

Log pile

If your shady corner is really tucked away or the neighbour's **leylandii** has totally shaded a corner of your garden, import a few large logs and create an artistic log pile . Decay is a vital part of the woodland habitat and the logs will provide a home for a wide range of fascinating plants and animals and many others will visit it looking for slugs and insects etc. Why not make a permanent home

Harts Tongue fern
Polypody Fern
Ivy
Moss
Liverwort
Ladyfern
Bracket Fungi
Fungi

for the local hedgehog here? Place the hedgehog house on a brick base and cover with polythene and leaves to ensure water cannot penetrate, then arrange the logs around it allowing one or two entrance *alleys* to the box. If left undisturbed there is a good chance it will be used. Place some damp sand along the *alleys* and you will be able to see who visits the box by footprints left in the sand.

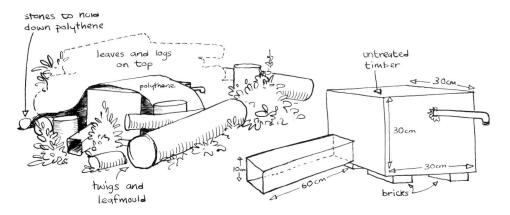

stones to hold down polythene
leaves and logs on top
polythene
untreated timber
30cm
30cm
30cm
twigs and leafmould
60cm
bricks

Creating a new shady (woodland) corner

Choose the place for your woodland corner carefully so you use the trees to enhance a good view or block an unsightly one. It should be away from buildings and ponds, and shouldn't make the sunniest part of your garden into a new shaded area!

Choosing the trees

There are several native trees suitable for a small garden, which are both attractive to us and excellent for wildlife. Select four or five including some that can be kept small by coppicing. The trees you select for coppicing should be allowed to grow and become established for about five years before the first cut. There after,cut every 7-10 years, or sooner if the tree is getting too large for the area. The *billhook* is the traditional coppicing tool, but we find a 50cm triangular bow saw is easier for the average gardener -especially on multiple-stemmed trees. Always do this work in winter,keeping yourself warm with the sawing, and the felled timber (firewood!).

Coppicing

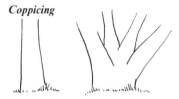

cut the stems as low as possible and with a slope to allow rain water to run off

Regular coppicing keeps the woodland floor open to allow wildflowers to flourish

New growth will re-generate from the cut stump

The diagram on pages 18 and 19 shows the new woodland corner created in one of our own gardens which is open to very cold north winds.The tree species were chosen with their wildlife value and tolerance to local conditions in mind. The taller tree species were planted towards the back with the smaller and coppiced trees nearer the front. They were planted about 2m apart - but if your corner is larger, spread them out more. **Silver birch** is a good choice for a standard tree in almost any situation as it is tolerant of all conditions, is readily available, relatively fast growing, and the dappled shade it casts is ideal for the growth of woodland flowers.

Other trees we recommend for gardens, as they tolerate most conditions and soil types, are **scots pine** (one of our native conifers) which also gives winter colour, **hazel** and **field maple** (for coppicing) and **rowan** (for its berries).

Below is a list of other trees and shrubs suitable for a woodland corner. Some prefer specific soil types but we have found them all to grow happily in the *normal* soil at our Centre.

For wetter soils: Alder; Buckthorn; Wild service tree; Guelder rose.
For chalky soils: Dogwood; Spindle; Whitebeam; Wayfaring tree; Wild privet (semi-evergreen); Bird cherry.
Most soil types: Dog rose; Elder (beware - invasive); Goat willow (fast growing - control by cutting back); Hawthorn; Holly; Crab apple.

If in doubt, look to see which types grow well in your area and choose these.

Buying your trees

Native trees are available from many nurseries - look up specialist *tree nurseries* in the yellow pages and try these first. We recommend you buy bare rooted plants (no soil on their roots) between November and March and plant them straight away. Make sure they have a good fibrous root system and that the roots look moist when you buy them. Try to get *transplants* (a one-year old plant transplanted for a further year) of heights 60-120cm as these establish readily and grow quickly. For a more instant effect, trees are available up to 2.5 metres tall, but these are more expensive and difficult to establish - suffering greater shock when transplanted, needing extra care and growing more slowly. The smaller trees soon catch up, and apart from anything else, they fit easily in your car!

You may need to plant outside the November-March period, or want evergreens. In this case, buy *container grown* specimens (grown in pots from seed). These transplant without much root disturbance, so larger trees may be used successfully, but they cost quite a lot more.

How to plant

Choose a day when the soil is not frozen or waterlogged. Start by clearing an area round the site of the tree about 1m diameter, removing any grass and weeds. Then dig a hole wide enough to take the roots of the tree and deep enough for the soil to reach the same level on the tree as in the nursery (this mark is easily seen on the stem). Break up the soil in the bottom of the hole with a fork, and if you have poor soil, work in a small amount of organic fertiliser. Mix it well - one level handful of an organic fertiliser such as concentrated chicken manure, blood, fish and bone or seaweed meal provides sufficient nutrients for the young tree.

If you have an exposed and windy site, trees over 1m tall will require staking and tying - put the stake in the hole *before* you plant the tree, so as to avoid root damage. Always stake on the *windward* side. Ask your local tree nursery about suitable stakes and ties.

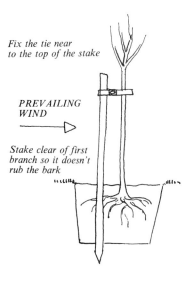

Fix the tie near to the top of the stake

PREVAILING WIND

Stake clear of first branch so it doesn't rub the bark

Until you are ready to plant the tree keep it in a plastic bag to help keep the roots moist. If they look dry, soak them in water for a few minutes. When you are ready for the tree, remove it from the bag and insert into the hole, carefully spreading the roots out. Fill with topsoil using a small amount initially and gently shake the tree up and down, then firm the soil gently with your foot. Continue filling and firming until the hole is full, the tree is vertical and the soil level just reaches the soil mark on the tree's stem.

Finally, if dry - water well with a good half-bucket of water for each tree and apply a mulch (this helps retain moisture and controls weed growth) immediately round the tree. The mulch might be a natural product - a 10cm layer of bark chippings or leaf mould - or man-made such as polythene mats.

9

Guarding and aftercare

Newly planted trees may be attacked by *rabbits*, so use a spiral rabbit guard - ask your nursery for advice. These expand as the tree grows and so may be left on for several years. In the garden, young trees can be *watered* regularly in dry weather: lack of water is the main cause of failure in young trees, so keep an eye on them. Mulching should ensure that **weed** competition is kept to a minimum, but you may need to help with some weeding in spring.

Some *pruning* may be necessary to remove crossing or broken branches, and to remove any dead or diseased parts (always burn these to avoid re-infection). Other than attending to the above, your trees should look after themselves, and the less they are tampered with, the more natural they will look.

Wildflowers for the new woodland corner

Unlike other wildflowers, shade loving plants require a richer soil, so try to imitate the floor of your nearest deciduous woodland - no need for any digging, just cover the soil with well rotted leaf mould if you have some, or one of the new peat-alternative products and plant into this. This should help conserve moisture too.

Leaf mould - the accumulation of rotted down dead leaves found on the woodland floor - can be made at home by collecting dead leaves and piling them up in a wire basket - they take about two years to rot down. Peat-alternatives, such as composted bark, coconut fibre, re-cycled cardboard and cocoa shells, also do the job of soil conditioning.

Use any of the wildflowers mentioned in this chapter but remember,because the trees will still be small and the amount of shade negligible, your wildflowers will grow rapidly and so should be planted well apart (30-45cm) and thinned out each year.

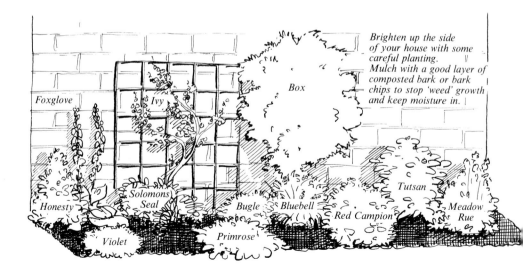

Brighten up the side of your house with some careful planting. Mulch with a good layer of composted bark or bark chips to stop 'weed' growth and keep moisture in.

Box

Foxglove

Ivy

Solomons Seal

Honesty

Violet

Primrose

Bugle

Bluebell

Red Campion

Tutsan

Meadow Rue

A well kept lawn can be a magnificent feature in the garden as a setting for the borders around it. However, well managed lawns are time consuming and for many of us a cut once a week in summer is usually all the attention we can give. It is important to have some short grass or other open space in order to sit and enjoy the garden, for the children to play on and for the birds to feed and display, but the alternatives to mown grass are much more exciting and the benefits for the local flora and fauna are obvious.

The wild flower meadow habitat is noticeably missing from our countryside today. Modern farming methods leave no place for the time consuming hay making of the past, and vigorous agricultural grasses for silage are preferred. But it was those old farming methods carried on for hundreds of years that provided ideal conditions for the wildflowers, butterflies and birds so associated with open grassy fields, and often so sadly missing today.

Whether you have a large or small lawn, a very positive contribution to conservation would be to convert part of this grassed area in to a small *wildflower meadow*. This involves leaving your lawn uncut for a certain period each year to let the grasses and wildflowers flower and set seed. How long you leave it and when to cut it depends on factors such as soil fertility and species composition and it is best to follow one of the cutting regimes shown next. When you choose, bear in mind your own lifestyle. For example, if you have children at home for the school holidays it may be preferable to choose a spring meadow to allow for the extra grass area in the summer months. Once you have mastered your particular management regime you will find you have plenty of time to sit back and enjoy it.

A: The spring flowering meadow

The spring meadow regime mimics the traditional hay meadow where a mixture of hay making in mid July and grazing enable a wide range of grasses and wild flowers to exist together . The summer and autumn grazing prevents the grasses growing excessively and dominating the sward, and also prevents scrub invasion. In a garden situation, the mower with a grass collector does a very good imitation *graze!*

JAN	FEB	MAR	APR	MAY	JUN	JUL	AUG	SEP	OCT	NOV	DEC

Cut in mid-july with scythe or strimmer

Leave the cut 'hay' to lie for 2 or 3 days

Once cut, keep at 7cms. tall for the rest of the summer. Use a rotary mower with a grass collector

B: The summer flowering meadow

In the far south of Britain it was possible to take two hay cuts in the year or the first flush of good grass in summer was used for grazing. This encouraged the later flowering meadow plants to flourish - such as **field scabious, black knapweed, yarrow** and **St Johns wort.** These flowers are generally taller but flower for a long period and are much loved by the later summer butterflies . Managing the *summer* meadow is slightly different from the *spring* meadow, because to prevent the strong growth of the grasses in early summer, you should cut it back to a height of 5cm each time it reaches 10cm. How often you will need to cut depends on the growing season, but it will be less often than for a formal lawn - saving work. Most garden mowers set at their highest cut will cope and will give the desired effect, but don't forget to remove all the cuttings each time. From mid-June put the mower away and leave the *lawn* to flower and set seed before you cut it again.

The meadow flowers and sets seed from July to October. Cut in mid-October using a scythe or strimmer. Leave cut hay for a day or two to allow seed to drop down into the sward. Then rake off the hay.

JAN FEB MAR APR MAY JUN JUL AUG SEP OCT NOV DEC

You may like to leave the meadow uncut over the winter months as you will find birds taking seeds from the flower heads, and insects hibernating amongst the grass stems. Alternatively you could cut half, and leave some uncut. Whichever you decide, you must cut and clear the hay before spring.

C: Single autumn cut

If your soil is poor and grass doesn't grow vigorously anyway, you may find that spring and summer cuts are not needed. In this case, choose from the whole meadow range of wildflowers (see below) and cut just once in the late autumn or winter.

The meadow flowers and sets seed from May to October. Cut in the autumn using a scythe or strimmer. Leave the cut hay for 2 or 3 days to enable seeds to drop down into the sward. Then remove the hay.

JAN FEB MAR APR MAY JUN JUL AUG SEP OCT NOV DEC

12

Creating your wildflower meadow - using pot grown wild flowers

Most ordinary garden soils are suitable for the introduction of a variety of wild flowers. Good results can be obtained by buying pot grown wildflowers and planting them out into the grass. First cut the grass very short and remove the clippings. Then select wild flowers suitable for your chosen cutting regime and place them on the grass in a random manner. Three or four of one kind in a group gives a natural look. Plant each 20 to 40 cm apart into the grass. Do not add fertiliser and remove a square of turf from each planting hole. This will help the plant to establish before the grass closes around it. Firm the plant in well, and keep it watered if the weather is dry. The best time for planting is the autumn (August - October) when the grasses have stopped actively growing but the soil is still warm enough for root growth.

It is a good idea to choose and plant just a few species in the first year, sticking to plants which cope with many situations -such as **oxeye daisy, musk mallow, sorrel** and **meadow buttercup**. Then, once you have had a year managing your meadow, you can increase the variety by choosing other plants which grow well in the wild with the varieties already established. You can also experiment with many other wild flowers. The chances of creating the very same environment as a 300 year old herb-rich meadow are (of course) poor, but with some careful management a very satisfying and beautiful wild flower meadow can result. You may also find that some of the local flora will seed itself into your meadow - a good sign that you are in tune with the environment.

*Common spotted orchids frequently **arrive** in newly created wildflower meadows*

Wildflowers to include in :

a spring flowering meadow
Oxeye daisy
Birdsfoot trefoil
Selfheal
Vipers bugloss
Salad burnet
Common vetch
Meadow buttercup
Cowslip
Sorrel
Yellow rattle
Ribwort plantain
Musk mallow

a summer flowering meadow
Oxeye daisy
Meadow buttercup
Field scabious
Black knapweed
Musk mallow
Wild carrot
Yarrow
Ribwort plantain
Meadow cranesbill
Goats beard

Creating your wildflower meadow - using seed

If your soil is fertile then it may be easier to begin your meadow from seed. This is also the best option if you are beginning a new garden from bare soil. Wildflowers seldom compete well against the common weeds and garden plants which thrive on good soil, so first you must reduce the fertility of your soil. Remove the turf and the soil that sticks to it, then either

Grow hungry vegetables for a year or two.	*or*	remove as much topsoil as you can from the whole site.

Once you have your low fertility soil, prepare the seed bed. Clear out any weeds and rake in to a fine even tilth. Then sow your seed. If you leave it for 2 or 3 weeks, weeds will appear which can be removed and the soil re-raked.

Several companies produce their own wildflower meadow mixtures (including School Garden Co. - see *Appendix*) and it is as well to scan the catalogues to find one which will suit your soil type and cutting regime. A general purpose mixture is suitable for any ordinary garden soil and will contain meadow grasses and wild flowers. Check if the grasses in the mixture include **red fescue, browntop, sheep's fescue, crested dogstail** and **smoooth meadow grass.** These grasses are attractive in flower and will not compete adversely with your wildflowers. Mixtures should contain about 80% grasses and 20% flower seeds.

The wild flowers should include a few species which adapt well to a wide range of conditions - such as **oxeye daisy , meadow buttercup ,sorrel, black knapweed , self heal** and **birds foot trefoil**. If your soil is well drained, sandy or stony, look for **field scabious, toadflax , musk mallow, cowslip , vetch, vipers bugloss** and **yellow rattle** as well. If you have a

Cowslip	**Musk Mallow**	**Small Scabious**	**Oxeye Daisy**
Allow to naturalise in a meadow area or flower border	*Long flowering period, musky scent and spikey foliage*	*If regularly dead-headed it will continue to flourish into December*	*Much loved by butterflies bees and hoverflies, easy to grow in a border or grassland*

moist soil or heavy clay, look for **ragged robin, fleabane, yellow rattle** and **devilsbit scabious**, and if very chalky, **kidney vetch, clustered bellflower, dropwort, cowslip**, and **wild marjoram**.

One of the important factors in producing a good wild flower meadow from seed is to sow at a very low rate - just 3 grammes per square metre. Work out the area of your patch, weigh the seed out carefully, then sow on a calm and cool day. We have found that it is sufficient just to firm the seed bed with a roller or by treading after sowing. If *raked*, the seeds may be buried too deep - after all, the natural way is for the seeds just to fall on the ground surface. If the soil is very dry, soak it first with a continuous fine spray. The best time for sowing is in the autumn, but it can also be done in spring. Water regularly in dry weather even after germination.

mix the seed with a large quantity of sand or sawdust. This helps to sow evenly

First year management involves cutting short for the whole of the first season, regardless of when sown. This encourages good strong root growth and well established plants in the second year. Cut your meadow when it reaches about 10cm, down to 5cm height. You can use a rotary mower for this, with a grass collector to remove the cut grass each time. You should be able to see the individual wild flowers and grasses in the sward and gradually they will join to form a continuous green cover. This *establishment* year also gives you a chance to see and remove any *weed* species that will still be there. Be careful that you identify these correctly! If in doubt, leave them to grow until you are certain.

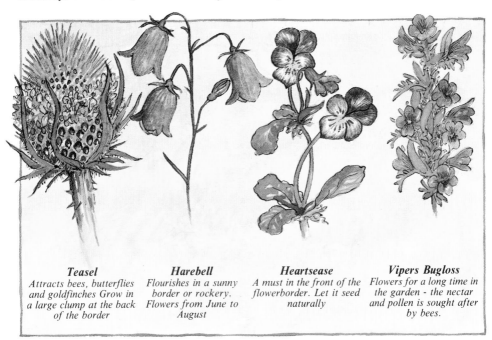

Teasel	*Harebell*	*Heartsease*	*Vipers Bugloss*
Attracts bees, butterflies and goldfinches Grow in a large clump at the back of the border	*Flourishes in a sunny border or rockery. Flowers from June to August*	*A must in the front of the flowerborder. Let it seed naturally*	*Flowers for a long time in the garden - the nectar and pollen is sought after by bees.*

In the **second year**, begin your chosen management regime. Don't worry if not all the wild flowers in your mixture show themselves at first. The flowering show varies from year to year depending on many factors, especially local weather conditions. Add more varieties if you like, but keep to the same management system.

Large lawns

If you have a large area you can really go to town with your wild flower meadows. After defining areas where you would like to see wild flowers, divide them up into both spring and summer flowering meadows. A wider variety of wildflowers can then be introduced and butterflies in particular will benefit from the continual nectar source and food supply for the caterpillars.

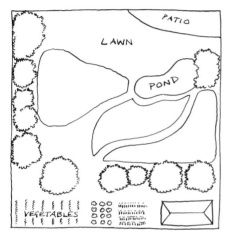

The spring meadow will be cut down by mid July so giving extra lawn for the summer. Mown pathways through and around the meadow are important both for your access, and to integrate the meadow areas into your garden scheme. Use hedges as a backdrop or a dense shrub border. You could include a small tree or a pond but keep your meadow areas away from flower borders.

Your weediest bits of lawn, on the poorest soil, will produce the best wild flower meadow. Once chosen, keep mowing the area (until you put in your meadow) and take off the clippings. Stop feeding this part of the lawn as it is not necessary.

Small lawns

If you have only a small area to set aside as a wild flower meadow it is best to decide on one form of management only. If you really have no area to give up to the meadow, try leaving the lawn uncut for a few weeks in summer. If when you look closely at your lawn, you see it is made up of grass but also many broad leaved plants as well - the common lawn *weeds* - you may need to do very little to turn this into a mini meadow.

Stop cutting the lawn in mid-June for a month and you will be surprised at the colourful show your lawn *weeds* will provide and how the local insect fauna will enjoy it too. Cut it down as soon as it begins to look untidy and resume normal mowing.

16

The late summer meadow

If you know your lawn is richly fertile and free of *weeds* but would still like to try a mini-meadow, then concentrate on the late summer meadow. Grass growth is most vigorous in the early months of summer and in such a fertile environment if allowed to grow, the grasses would quickly dominate any wild flowers added. By carefully selecting your wild flowers and managing the meadow correctly you can create an attractive late summer show.

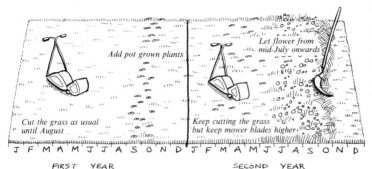

The shady meadow

Lawn grasses often grow very poorly under the shade of trees, walls, fences and these natural gaps in grass cover offer ideal sites to add in pot grown wild flowers. Choose species which will mimic a woodland edge or hedgerow - **red campion, wood avens, herbrobert, toadflax. agrimony,** and **betony** will all grow happily in a shaded meadow situation. Choose your cutting regime and manage your meadow as before.

The specialist meadow

Another attractive addition to the garden, very satisfying to create and with wild flower conservation in mind, is the specialist meadow. Many of our meadow flowers are now very rare so you may enjoy growing some of these plants. A word of warning: **never** take wild flowers from the wild, and **never** knowingly spread your garden wildflowers into the general countryside. Both these activities harm our wild flower stocks, and may be illegal.

See *Appendix* for availability of seed. Try growing **cowslips** with **snakeshead fritillary, harebells** with **ladies bedstraw, clustered bellflower** with **meadow vetchling** or **quaking grass** with **yellow rattle** and **betony.** Keep your choices simple.

In all cases choose a sunny spot. Size is not important. Remove the existing turf and topsoil, sow a meadow grass that compliments your chosen plants, at a low rate of 2gm per square metre. Wait until the grass has had its first cut, then plant pot grown plants of your selected species into gaps in the grass. Cut it short for the first year but allow to flower at the correct time in the second year, mowing early and again after taking off the hay crop. Remember not to mow lower than 5cm for the maintenance cuts. To make your mini-meadow stand out and look neat, keep the area round it close mown.

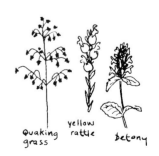

The Woodland Corner

Bird cherry (coppiced)
attractive flowers - good for
insects - berries eaten by
many small birds and
mammals

Robin
nest box

Daffodills

Do buy native bulbs
and wildflowers - not
imported ones

Aconite

Lungwort

5.

4.

1.

Sweet Violet

Primrose

Bugle

Dog Violet

keep this edge
close mown

1. Stinking Hellebore
2. Yellow Archangel
3. Greater Stitchwort
4. Wild Strawberry
5. Lords and Ladies
6. Red Campion
7. Soapwort
8. Honeysuckle

9. Comfrey
10. Gt. Mullein Aaron's Rod
11. Foxglove
12. Sweet Rocket
13. Columbine
14. Herb Robert
15. Wood Avens
16. Red Campion

17. Bluebell
18. Lady Fern
19. Woodruff

20. Hazel (coppiced)
makes a multi-stemmed shrub.
Good for nesting birds.
Attractive catkins and nuts.

18   *Plant in large drifts of one species (but as many early flowering bulbs as you like)
and remember that some will need cutting down after flowering and all will need
a tidy-up in the autumn.*

Birch
insects
finches
the seeds

Scots Pine
attracts long-tailed tits
and goldcrests

Bat box

Holly
make sure that you buy
a female. thrushes
and blackbirds love
the berries.

9.

10.

11.

Concentrate the
taller flowers at
the back

12.

13

Hazel

14

17.

15

18

19

Snowdrop

Primrose

Sweet Violet

19

The patio is an integral part of most gardens today. As well as putting out tables and chairs, why not add some containers of wild flowers? They grow to their full potential when not in competition with other species. Grow some in pots, as a pretty and different way of decorating your patio, and a valuable food source for insects and birds too.

Which containers to use

Wildflowers will grow in most containers, but they probably look best in natural materials. For example, try old wooden barrels, terracotta pots, old chimney pots or old stone sinks. Whatever containers you choose, make sure they have drainage holes (except for a bog garden or pond) so the soil does not become waterlogged - roots must breathe!

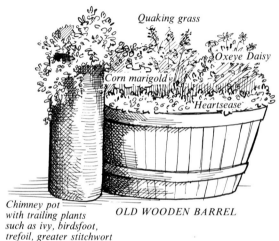

Quaking grass

Oxeye Daisy

Corn marigold

Heartsease

Chimney pot with trailing plants such as ivy, birdsfoot, trefoil, greater stitchwort

OLD WOODEN BARREL

To create a *miniature pond* or a *bog garden*, choose a water-tight tub - half an old wooden barrel is again ideal. Soak it for a few days so that it will swell and seal any leaks. Or choose a pot and line it with plastic. For *hanging baskets*, the traditional wire basket lined with moss looks more natural with wildflowers than a plastic non-drip version.

The dimensions of a container are not important: a large tub can hold a mixture of plants or smaller tubs might be planted with individual species and grouped together on the patio.

Which compost to use

Don't use garden soil as this will contain the seeds of many weeds which will soon compete with the wildflowers. Any ordinary potting compost will do but we recommend a soil based compost as it is heavier (giving the pot more stability) and is less liable to waterlogging. *John Innes No.2 compost* is the one to look for in garden centres. It contains some nutrients but these will be used up by the growing plants in the first few months, so the regular use of an organic fertiliser (try seaweed meal) will prolong flowering and ensure the plants' survival. If you want acid-loving plants (heather, rock rose) buy a compost formulated specifically for this - usually called *ericaceous compost*.

Which plants to use

The choice of plants depends on the situation. Plants whose natural habitat is woodland will be suitable for a shady corner of the patio. Meadow, coastal and upland plants prefer lots of sun. (Remember plants in pots in full sun need watering regularly). A container with no drainage holes will suit plants that grow along the edges of streams or other boggy places. Page 22 will give you some ideas to start with, or use other designs in this book.

Plants selected for ease of availability and/or easy growth from seed.

Low Growing & Creeping	Medium Height	Tall
Birdsfoot-trefoil	Clustered bellflower	Foxglove
* Heartsease	Cowslip	Dark mullein
Primrose	* Feverfew	Teasel
Rockrose	* Forget-me-not	Small scabious
Tufted vetch	* Oxeye daisy	* Corncockle
Violet	* Red poppy	* Black knapweed
* Wild strawberry	Quaking grass	* Corn marigold
Yellow archangel	Soapwort	
* Thrift		**Shade**
Pasque flower	**Marsh**	Violet
* Red clover	* Ragged robin	* Red campion
* Kidney vetch	* Forget-me-not	* Herb robert
Biting stonecrop	* Monkey flower	Gt. stitchwort
Wild thyme	Water mint	Ferns
* Herb robert	Ladys smock	Wild daffodil
Gt stitchwort	Marsh marigold	Wild strawberry
Ladies bedstraw		Foxglove
		Primrose
		Cyclamen

* should flower the same year from a spring sowing

Designing your mini-nature-reserve is fairly simple - choose plants that grow together in the same habitat and fit in with the scale of the container. Consider the continuity of flowering - the wrong selection could mean you get a spectacular show for a week or two and then nothing. Check flowering times on labels and choose one or two early-flowering plants such as **cowslip** (bought as a plant) and **fritillary** (bulb).

When you plant these, sow seeds of the cornfield annuals, which will give you colour throughout the summer. Apart from these annuals, it is best to buy pot-grown plants or to raise your own from seed (see Chapter 7) and then plant them out. If you sow seed in autumn, you should have strong plants ready to flower the following summer. Some will flower from a spring sowing - pop these into gaps. Try **heartsease, feverfew, forget-me-not, oxeye daisy** and **herb robert** (and those indicated * on the above list).

If you have several containers, plant with individual species that look good together. Then you can move them around, or out of the way, as their colours change or fade. Prepare some with just flowering grasses, ferns and attractive foliage which will contrast with the flowers. Grasses suitable for containers include **cotton grass, wall barley, cats tail, meadow foxtail, wavy hair grass, Yorkshire fog, quaking grass** and **wild oats**.

How do I plant?

Once you have chosen your plants, prepare the container. Cover the drainage holes with a layer of flat stones or broken clay pot. If you have selected chalk-loving species, cover this stone layer with limestone chippings, and for other species use a layer of pea gravel. Then put in a layer of leaf mould before filling with a suitable compost. For a containerised *bog garden* omit the flat stones (there should be no drainage holes) and increase the amount of leaf mould to help with moisture retention.

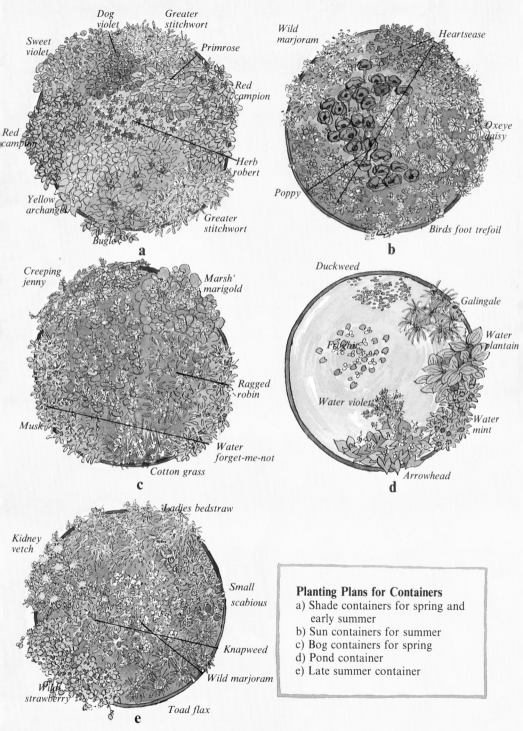

a)
Sweet violet
Dog violet
Greater stitchwort
Primrose
Red campion
Red campion
Herb robert
Yellow archangel
Greater stitchwort
Bugle

b)
Wild marjoram
Heartsease
Oxeye daisy
Poppy
Birds foot trefoil

c)
Creeping jenny
Marsh marigold
Ragged robin
Musk
Water forget-me-not
Cotton grass

d)
Duckweed
Galingale
Water plantain
Water violet
Water mint
Arrowhead

e)
Ladies bedstraw
Kidney vetch
Small scabious
Knapweed
Wild strawberry
Wild marjoram
Toad flax

Planting Plans for Containers
a) Shade containers for spring and early summer
b) Sun containers for summer
c) Bog containers for spring
d) Pond container
e) Late summer container

Trellis, walls and fences - (vertical gardening)

Hops
Both male and female plants required. Quick growing and self supporting. The attractive leaves climb clockwise and the 'hops' on the female plant in autumn are strongly scented. Just tie in the stems where necessary.

Honeysuckle
Likes some support especially at first. Tie to trellis or wires. Wonderful scent on a midsummer evening and birds love the berries in autumn.

Thrushes enjoy rose hips

Moths feed on honeysuckle flowers

Need some support and pruning in winter. Can produce a wonderful dense tangle if only lightly pruned. Nest sites for birds, nectar for insects and rosehips in winter.

Trellis

Fence

Dog rose

Wood Vetch
A good climber with attractive flowers, will scramble up the stems of other climbers or a trellis.

Sweet briar

To provide a dense screen plant only 30cms. apart.

Use a rustic trellis to hang bird feeders in winter and net bags of animal hair in spring.

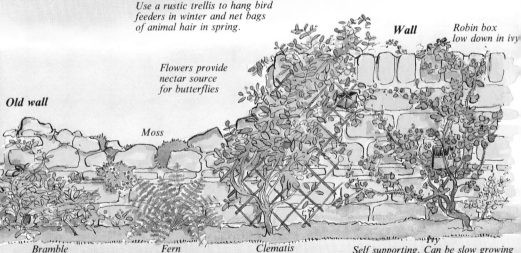

Wall **Robin box**
low down in ivy

Flowers provide nectar source for butterflies

Old wall

Moss

Bramble **Fern** **Clematis**

Self supporting. Can be slow growing initially. Attractive flowers and berries in autumn and winter. Evergreen. Insects like to hibernate behind the leaves and the berries and an important food source for birds in late winter.

Ivy

Lots of gaps for hibernating newts, frogs and toads

Spotted flycatcher box on ledge behind trellis.

You can have a lot of fun covering vertical surfaces with native climbing plants. For best effect give them lots of space.

23

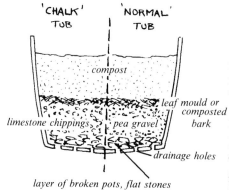

'CHALK' TUB | 'NORMAL' TUB

compost

leaf mould or composted bark

limestone chippings | pea gravel

drainage holes

layer of broken pots, flat stones

Now plant the flowers - try haphazard groupings of one species rather than rows, and let the plants find their own space. Many will flop over the edge and still flower quite happily. Most wildflowers respond to dead-heading by producing another flower, so it is worth spending a little time doing this to prolong the show.

Miniature pond

Fill the bottom of your chosen watertight container with a 6 to 8cm layer of sand and gravel. Then fill with water (about 45cm deep), but wait 48 hours before planting. As there is no soil in which to put the pond plants, keep them in containers and cut back when they begin to grow strongly. Five or six plants will be sufficient for a half-barrel or large tub. Select these from the list below and keep them in their original pots - make sure the compost is well soaked and is soil based as peat tends to float away! Put a layer of fine gravel on top of the compost. Some plants will be happy if the pots are just placed on the gravel bottom but stand marginals on bricks so that the soil in their pots is *just* covered by water. As always, select a mixture of tall and short species.

Submerged (pots on gravel): Water crowfoot; Water violet; Mares tail; Arrowhead; Water plantain; Water starwort; Hornwort.
Marginals (pots on bricks): Water mint; Water forget-me-not; Ragged robin; Marsh marigold; Bog bean; Brooklime.

Finally, put in some oxygenating plants such as **hornwort** or **water milfoil**, add a few snails and the rest of the wildlife will arrive naturally.

Hanging baskets

These require a bit more preparation. For wire baskets, line the base with some damp (living) spaghnum moss, green side outwards and secure it with some compost. Gradually build up the side with more moss, adding flowers through this and the wire as you go, securing the roots by filling the basket with compost. Leave room for one or two upright plants in the centre. Whichever trailing plants you choose, pinching out the growing tips occasionally will promote bushy growth. Don't forget to water in dry weather.

Upright plants in centre of basket

Trailing plant around edge

WIRE BASKET LINED WITH MOSS AND COMPOST

Birdsfoot trefoil — Red Clover
Feverfew
Hearsease — Wild strawberry
Tufted vetch
Wild thyme

PLANTING SCHEME TO TRY

Wildflowers of open fields, cliffs and woodland glades are equally at home in a sunny or partially sunny spot in the garden so include some in your herbaceous border, around ponds or on a rockery. You can even create a border full of colour and all year interest using *only* wildflowers. They produce the pollen, nectar and seed which is sought after by a huge variety of insects, birds and animals. Far from creating a static display of colour (so typical of many parks) you can discover this whole new bustling world by simply planting your favourite wildflowers. Remember, butterflies and other insects are like us and prefer the best parts of the garden, so if your garden is exposed to the wind, put a trellis or fence around the borders - see *page 23*.

You might combine wildflowers with traditional garden plants, especially if working to a colour scheme. Our experience is that most wildflowers combine well with the old fashioned cottage garden flowers and herbs which are little changed from their wild state. In fact, many are wildflowers from another country. In contrast, some modern garden flowers have been so altered by plant breeders to produce large, very decorative or brightly coloured blooms that their value as a food source for insects and birds is very limited or non-existent. Don't be too worried about matching the wildflowers to soil type - all the easily available wildflowers adapt well to any normal garden soil and grow much stronger, as the soil has more nutrients and the plants have less competition from grasses.

Wildflower island border

Island borders (in lawns or paved areas) are usually in full sun. If starting a new border, try planting it *all* with wildflowers - it will certainly be a talking point! Avoid placing all the tall flowers in the centre and include some with interesting foliage as well as flowers - the **mulleins, tansy, vetch, thistles, columbine, sweet cicely** and **meadow rue** are good examples.

Rock Gardens - *artificial hillsides*

Prepare the slope with a base of rubble/gravel topped with an 8cm soil based compost with added grit. It must be well drained.

Rock
Arrange the rocks to resemble a natural outcrop and leave gaps for planting.

Scree
Prepare the base as before. Place one or two large rocks on the slope then a series of smaller ones. Use rock chippings in between. Plant in gravel and scree with a crowbar and trowel to make a hole. backfill with good soil, insert the plant and cover soil with gravel or chippings.

Gravel
Try and match gravel to the colour of the rocks. Rock steps make a feature - angle them into the slope for safety and infill gaps with gravel.

Waterfall
Everyone enjoys running water, including birds and mamals. Pre-formed waterfall pieces never really match your rocks, so butyl rubber may be a better choice. Cover as much as possible with rock and gravel. Leave an overhang at the edge of each pool. You will need a pump and electricity for the water to flow.

1. Red campion	10. Wild thyme	19. Bog bean
2. Yellow horned poppy	11. Jacob's ladder	20. Ragged robin
3. Alpine lady's mantle	12. Heather	21. Cotton grass
4. Mountain avens	13. Birds-eyed primrose	22. Fern
5. Bloody cranesbil	14. Rock rose	23. Water avens
6. Chamomile	15. Pasque flower	24. Forget-me-not
7. Centaury	16. Clustered bellflower	25. Herb robert
8. Biting stonecrop	17. Flax	26. Bog asphodel
9. Thrift	18. Harebell	

All year round wildflower border

Here you can really go to town. Choose from your favourites and come up with a planting plan to give you some interest from the first snowdrops in January to the last **scabious, wild carrot** and **yarrow** flower of the autumn. If you have a large border, plant individual species in groups of 5 or more, about 20cm apart. Try to put the taller species at the back of the border, medium height species in the middle and low growing species to the front, perhaps varied with one or two large plants at the front.

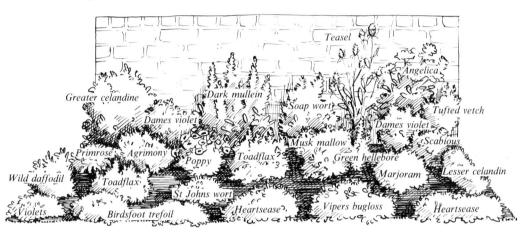

Combining wildflowers and herbs

Wildflowers and herbs mix beautifully together. Have fun with colour combinations as in this **"Blue" bee and butterfly border**:

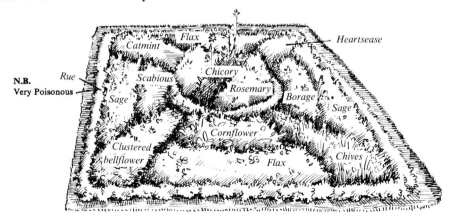

Wildflowers with herbaceous garden plants

A *cottage* style border close to your house will give much pleasure and is an ideal feeding station for wildlife. Mix perennials, biennials and annuals and allow them to seed themselves, removing excess seedlings.

27

Suggested border plants

Our choice of cottage garden plants

Evening primrose	Sunflower	Delphinium
Crocus	Mallow	Lupin
Grape hyacinth	Golden rod	Pot marigold
Polyanthus	Phlox	Nasturtium
White arabis	Globe thistle	Verbena
Honesty	Sea holly	Allysum
Aubretia	Cosmos	Wallflower
Michaelmas daisy	Forget-me-not	Sweet william
Perennial cornflower	Poppy	Large daisies
Geraniums	Poached egg plant	Californian poppy
Tobacco plant	Mignonette	Yarrow
Hollyhock	Snapdragon	Ice plant

Plant the *single flowered* types for their nectar.

Wildflowers for a sunny border

	TALL	MEDIUM	SHORT
YELLOW	Gt celandine Weld (B) Evening primrose (B) Gt mullein (B) Dark mullein (B) Golden rod Tansy	Meadow buttercup Welsh poppy St John's wort Tutsan Agrimony Toadflax Corn marigold (A)	Lesser celandine Birds foot trefoil Kidney vetch Primrose Cowslip Wild daffodil
PURPLE	Meadow cranesbill Tufted vetch Jacobs ladder Foxglove (B) Spear thistle Hedge woundwort	Marjoram Betony Selfheal Black knapweed	Pasque flower Snakes head fritillary Wild thyme
BLUE	Columbine Vipers bugloss Nettle leaved bell flower Teasel Small scabious Field scabious Chicory Green alkanet	Clustered bellflower Cornflower (A)	Perennial flax Common dog violet Sweet violet Heartsease (A) Harebell
WHITE	Meadow rue Dames violet Sweet cicely Angelica (B) Wild carrot Comfrey	White campion (A) Gt stitchwort Dropwort Oxeye daisy Feverfew (A) White dead nettle	Wood amemone Wild strawberry Meadow saxifrage
RED/PINK	Corncockle (A) Gt knapweed	Poppy (A) Deptford pink (A) Soapwort Red campion Musk Mallow	Wood anemone Herb robert Thrift
GREEN		Green hellebore Stinking hellebore Salad burnett Woodspurge	Perennials unless marked (A) Biennial (B) Annual

The above grow well in good garden soil. If you have *acid* or *calcareous* soil, try the plants below:

Acid soils

Bluebell, birdsfoot trefoil, dog violet, rockrose, betony, sheeps sorrel, foxglove (B), heather, bilberry, woodsage, devils bit scabious.

Calcareous soils

Pasque flower, bladder campion, columbine, salad burnet, cowslip, rockrose, harebell, dropwort, wild thyme, quaking grass.

Pond and marsh plants

There are many lovely wetland wild flowers to choose from, but a word of warning. Don't buy too many to begin with as most increase at a fantastic rate, so be prepared to thin out every year. We suggest planting all the short to medium height types together, and the medium to tall types together. This way the taller (and more dominant) types won't swamp the lower creeping types.

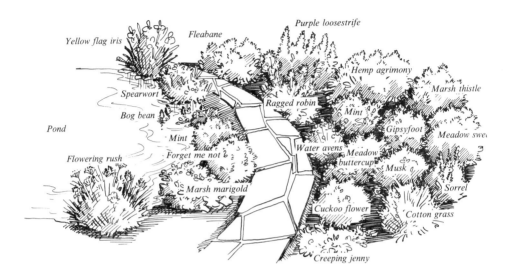

Plant no closer than 30cm if short growing species, and up to 45cm if taller or creeping types.

Golden rules

1. Choose plants to give some interest throughout the year and to provide pollen and nectar. Dead head (cut off faded flower heads) to increase the flowering period, leaving some flower heads to seed towards the end of the season. Then remove dead stems and tidy up.

2. Take note of plant size. In good soil, many wildflowers grow stronger and taller and so their border position needs thought. Use the maximum height given in field guides.

3. Most wildflowers have subtle colours, and so blend well with each other, making colour matching unnecessary. Plant in groups; leave some to seed each year; enjoy the haphazard arrangements they produce, but remove those in the wrong place.

4. Fertilise only as autumn dressing, unless your soil is poor. Then add organic fertiliser when planting and mid-way through the year.

5. Don't use pesticides or herbicides - be organic for the birds and insects! This can cause problems - our great mullein plants looked absolutely magnificent until we spotted holes in their leaves. Within a few days they were covered with caterpillars of the mullein moth and a dilemma arose. However, as the caterpillars were a talking point and highly attractive, we left them to consume the plants. We still had the flowers to look at.

6   Other garden sites for wildflowers

Herb gardens

We have already mentioned herbs in conjunction with wildflowers, but some wildflowers are *herbs* themselves - they have medicinal, culinary, fragrance and dye properties. So these could be incorporated into a formal herb garden. Many wildflowers were widely used in days gone by, and some continue to be used today as interest in homeopathy grows.

Here is our selection of suitable wildflowers/herbs:

Edible: Salad burnet; Elecampane; Wild strawberry; Sweet Cicely; Wild marjoram; Sorrel; Good King Henry.
Medicinal: Selfheal;. Meadowsweet; Centuary; St John's wort.
Perfumery: Sweet woodruff; Ladies bedstraw; Meadowsweet.
Dye: Soapwort; Dyers greenweed.

Vegetable gardens

Apart from growing some wildflowers as an edible crop, there is a place for some wildflowers in the vegetable garden as part of your pest control programme. Obviously if you are taking positive action to attract wildlife to your garden there is no room for chemical pesticides and herbicides - which may destroy the very things you are trying to attract. However, you still do not want cabbage white butterflies eating your brassicas or aphids swarming over the broad beans. There is no room here to cover the subject of organic pest control but if you have a garden full of wildflowers, herbs and cottage garden plants, the chances are that the natural enemies of your vegetable pests are in profusion and will deal with large numbers of them with no extra effort by you.

Hoverflies and their larvae are voracious eaters of aphids

You could try growing wildflowers alongside your vegetables for two reasons:

1. There is some evidence that root secretions have a beneficial effect on the soil enabling your vegetables to take up nutrients more effectively.

2. The flowers positively attract predators and may be used to disguise the crop from the air. Cornfield annuals seem to be best at this. Their growth is rapid and if carefully placed (so that they don't compete with the crop) they will make your vegetable garden more attractive too. Just make sure you remove the flowers before the seed ripens!

Hoverflies on corn marigold

Hedges

There is nothing like a native hedgerow, full of wild shrubs and trees, climbing plants and with wildflowers beneath. It provides a home for hundreds of living things. You may have such a hedge, but often these have been ripped out and replaced by a single species hedge - for the sake of tidiness!! Even so, you can still add wildflowers under it. The diagram gives some ideas for plants, and many will appear without your help, of course.

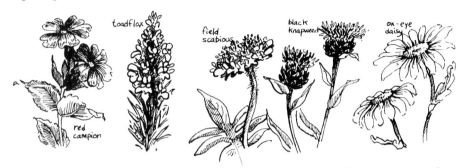

Whether you have grass under the hedge as well is up to you. If you want to, choose a meadow-type mixture and sow and manage it as shown in *chapter 3*. You might instead choose to treat the hedge bottom as a wildflower border. There are plenty of species to choose from, and you might include grasses as specimen plants. Just remember that it is often very dry under an established hedge, so the soil may need extra organic matter. Try *losing* your grass cuttings here - they make an excellent mulch.

Orchards

If you have an area set aside as an orchard, adding wildflowers will help attract insects vital to the pollination of your fruit blossom. Which to choose depends on how closely spaced the trees are. With an old orchard of large trees, treat as a *shady area* (see *chapter 2*) but with an open and grassy orchard, treat as a *lawn* (see *chapter 3*). It will help to locate one or two wildflower borders on the sunny side of the orchard, again to attract insects. Cornfield annuals are ideal for this.

Bats, birds and butterflies

Other books in this series give detailed help if you want to attract birds, or butterflies or bats into your garden. Each has planting ideas and plans to help make your dreams come true - see the *Appendix* for the book titles.

31

Many garden centres now stock pot grown wildflowers, but unfortunately in a very limited range and at a price that makes buying enough to stock your garden a very expensive exercise. Once you have drawn up your plans and put together a list of wildflowers you want, you can guarantee that you won't be able to find all the plants. Do not despair! You have two options:

1. Find a specialist nursery who grow a wide range and who supply by mail order. (See *Appendix* and gardening magazines; your county *Naturalist Trust* may also be able to help.)

2. Grow your own plants from seed. This is readily available by mail order (again see *Appendix*) and in a vast range of species. This approach is also much cheaper.

A word of warning ...
Under the *Wildlife and Countryside Act 1981*, it is an offence to uproot any wildflower (even the humble daisy!) unless you have the authority of the landowner. Some species are fully protected and cannot be picked or uprooted under any circumstances - so don't be tempted to get your plants from the countryside. Seed collecting from the wild is frowned upon, as the wild plants rely on their own seed for survival. Be safe and buy your plants and seed from recognised nurserymen. Make sure the plants and seeds you buy are truly British - that is the only way you can ensure you get the types you want.

Wildflowers from seed

It makes sense to sow the seed of perennial wildflowers in seed trays, rather than scatter it straight on the ground. Some species require special conditions for germination, or have irregular germination, or if they do emerge are painstakingly removed - as weeds!

Sowing the seed
Many wildflower seeds undergo *dormancy* changes during storage and will only germinate when conditions are right. We often have to wait for a year for some seeds to germinate, so don't give up or throw the compost away. One or two species require special treatment to release them from dormancy. Read the instructions on the seed packet just in case!

Scarification is a natural abrasive process, which normally occurs in the crops of birds. If your seed requires it, mimic this by rubbing the seed between two pieces of sandpaper or by making a small nick in the seed coat. This allows moisture into the seed to begin the germination process. All of the **pea** and **cranesbill** family will require this treatment.

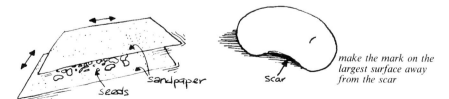

seeds

sandpaper

scar

make the mark on the largest surface away from the scar

Stratification - some seeds need a period of cold temperatures to encourage germination, from one to six months. Sow the seed in a tray in late summer or early autumn, cover with glass and leave in a cold frame or unheated greenhouse or just somewhere sheltered outdoors. Uncover when you see the first signs of germination and bring into a warmer area. Seeds of many woodland plants require this treatment, such as **primroses, cowslips, violets, poppies** and members of the **carrot** family.

When and how to sow indoors

Autumn and spring are the natural sowing times and it is best to stick to these. Sow perennial species in a seed tray of moist, soil-based compost, such as *John Innes Seed* or *No.1 Compost*, sowing small seeds on the surface and pushing larger ones just below the surface. Ensure a steady temperature and keep moist by placing a sheet of glass over the tray or putting the whole tray into a plastic bag.

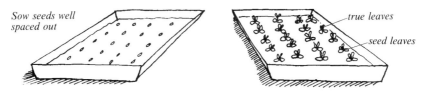

When the seedlings are large enough to handle, usually when they have at least two or three true leaves, gently remove each one and transplant either to individual pots (4-6cm diameter) or space out well in another seed tray filled with potting compost. Strong plants require good root systems so check for roots emerging from the holes in the trays or pots *before* planting out in the garden.

Usually perennials sown in the spring should be planted out in the autumn of the same year, flowering the next year. Our plants are all raised in the greenhouse and taken outside two weeks before planting out. Wildflowers are hardy but need a gentle introduction to strong winds, rain and cold if you have raised them in a sheltered environment. When planting out, firm the soil around each plant and water well if the soil is dry.

Sowing outdoors

Annual wildflowers - some annuals such as **heartsease (pansy)** will seed themselves many times during the summer. Others taller species tend to flop, seed very freely and require cultivated soil, making it easier to grow them together in one area. Sow these where they are to flower. Choose a sunny site with some shelter and preferably where the soil is well drained and nutritionally poor. In spring, sow a mixture of **common poppy, corn marigold, corn chamomile, corncockle, cornflower** and **heartsease**. Sow thinly over the surface and lightly rake in. (A mixture of cornfield annuals like this can be bought ready to sow.)

Water well with a fine spray, regularly if the soil is dry. With little other work, you will be rewarded with a stunning display of colour for several summer months. Cut them for the vase, and the display lasts even longer! At the end of the summer, pull up the dead stems and shake any seeds into the soil. Fork over and you will be ready for next year's display. If you are really clever, you can let the seed dry on the plants and collect your own mixture for the following season. There will be more seed than you need, but this should be in great demand from neighbours and friends.

Perennial wildflowers - if you want to sow perennials into the garden, choose a time in early spring or late summer/early autumn when the soil is warm and germination and seedling establishment will be rapid. Prepare the soil well, by digging and removing any weeds. Mark out the beds and label them so it is clear where one variety stops and another starts. Rake the soil to a fine tilth and mark out drills, no more than 1 cm deep, in straight lines or curves. Allow about 30cm between drills for hoeing.

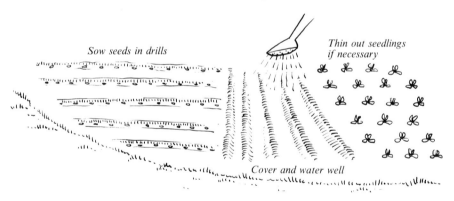

Sow seeds in drills   *Thin out seedlings if necessary*

Cover and water well

Sow the seed thinly in the drills and lightly cover. Water regularly during the germination period, if the soil is prone to drying out. At the seedling stage, thin out some of your plants as necessary and keep the soil hoed between them. Pinch out the leading shoots of your plants when they reach 10cm tall. This will produce strong bushy plants ready for flowering the next season.

Dividing plants

Your perennial wildflowers will increase in growth size each year but some will slow down after about three years. Divide plants in the dormant season (autumn and winter) by carefully digging up, shaking off any soil and then gently pulling it apart (you may need to use a knife or garden fork) so that each piece has roots and at least one shoot or bud. Re-plant each piece carefully and water in if the soil is dry.